AF599090

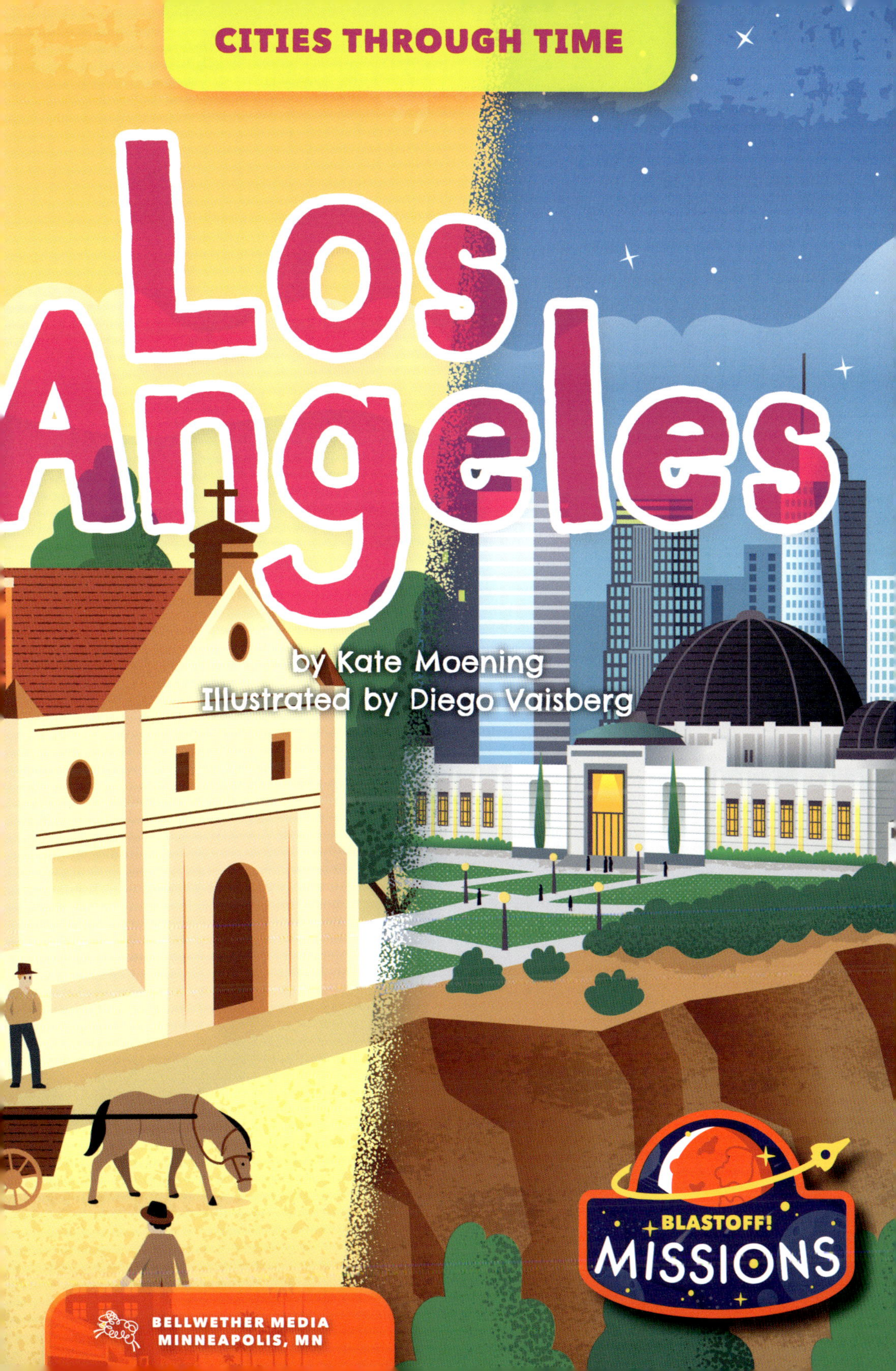
CITIES THROUGH TIME
Los Angeles
by Kate Moening
Illustrated by Diego Vaisberg
BLASTOFF!
MISSIONS
BELLWETHER MEDIA
MINNEAPOLIS, MN

Blastoff! Missions takes you on a learning adventure! Colorful illustrations and exciting narratives highlight cool facts about our world and beyond. Read the mission goals and follow the narrative to gain knowledge, build reading skills, and have fun!

Traditional Nonfiction

Narrative Nonfiction

Blastoff! Universe

MISSION GOALS

- FIND YOUR SIGHT WORDS IN THE BOOK.
- LEARN ABOUT DIFFERENT PERIODS IN LOS ANGELES'S HISTORY.
- LEARN ABOUT WHY PEOPLE HAVE COME TO LOS ANGELES THROUGH THE YEARS.

This edition first published in 2025 by Bellwether Media, Inc.

Library of Congress Cataloging-in-Publication Data

LC record for Los Angeles available at: https://lccn.loc.gov/2024046808

Editor: Christina Leaf   Designer: Laura Sowers

Printed in the United States of America, North Mankato, MN.

This is **Blastoff Jimmy**! He is here to help you on your mission and share fun facts along the way!

Table of Contents

Welcome to Los Angeles! ... 4
Life on the River ... 6
Government Changes ... 8
The City Grows ... 12
The City Today ... 20
Glossary ... 22
To Learn More ... 23
Beyond the Mission ... 24
Index ... 24

Welcome to Los Angeles!

Los Angeles, California, is always busy! More than 12 million people live in and around the city.

People love the sunny weather and beaches in L.A. Let's check out its past!

Life on the River

1500s

Here, the Tongva people live in Yaanga. This village is near today's Los Angeles River.

The people have hunted, fished, and traded here for centuries.

Los Angeles
River

Government Changes

A **mission** is near the river. The Spanish **governor** of California wants a new town, too. He offers free land to anyone who comes.

A group of 44 people starts Los Angeles!

1822
Mexico won **independence** from Spain last year! Mexico now governs Los Angeles.
ranch

Ranchers will come to the area. They will build huge ranches to raise cattle.

The City Grows

1876

California now belongs to the United States! A new railroad runs to Los Angeles. It is easier for people to get to the city.

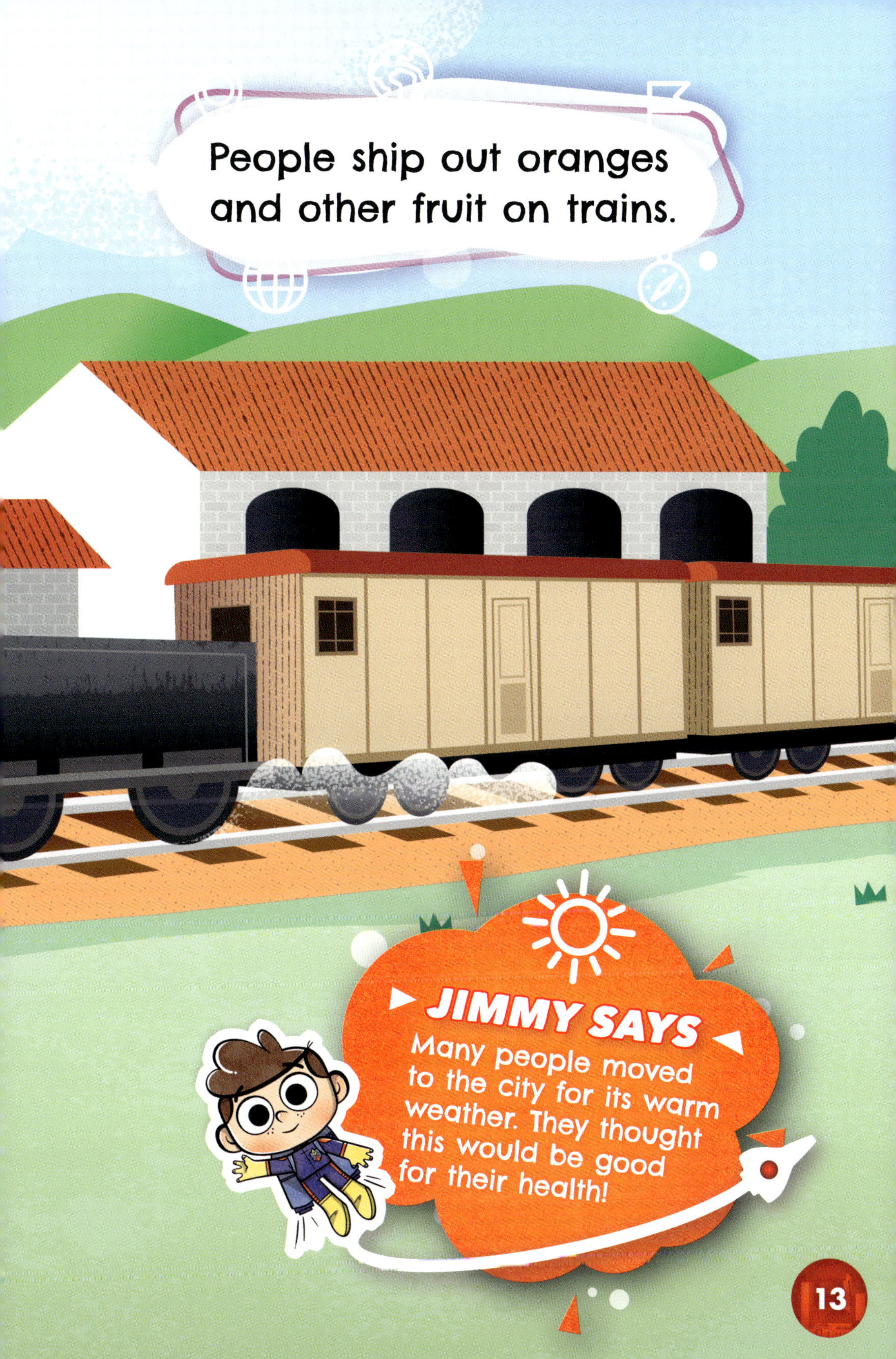
People ship out oranges and other fruit on trains.
JIMMY SAYS
Many people moved to the city for its warm weather. They thought this would be good for their health!

1920s
The movie business is booming in Los Angeles!

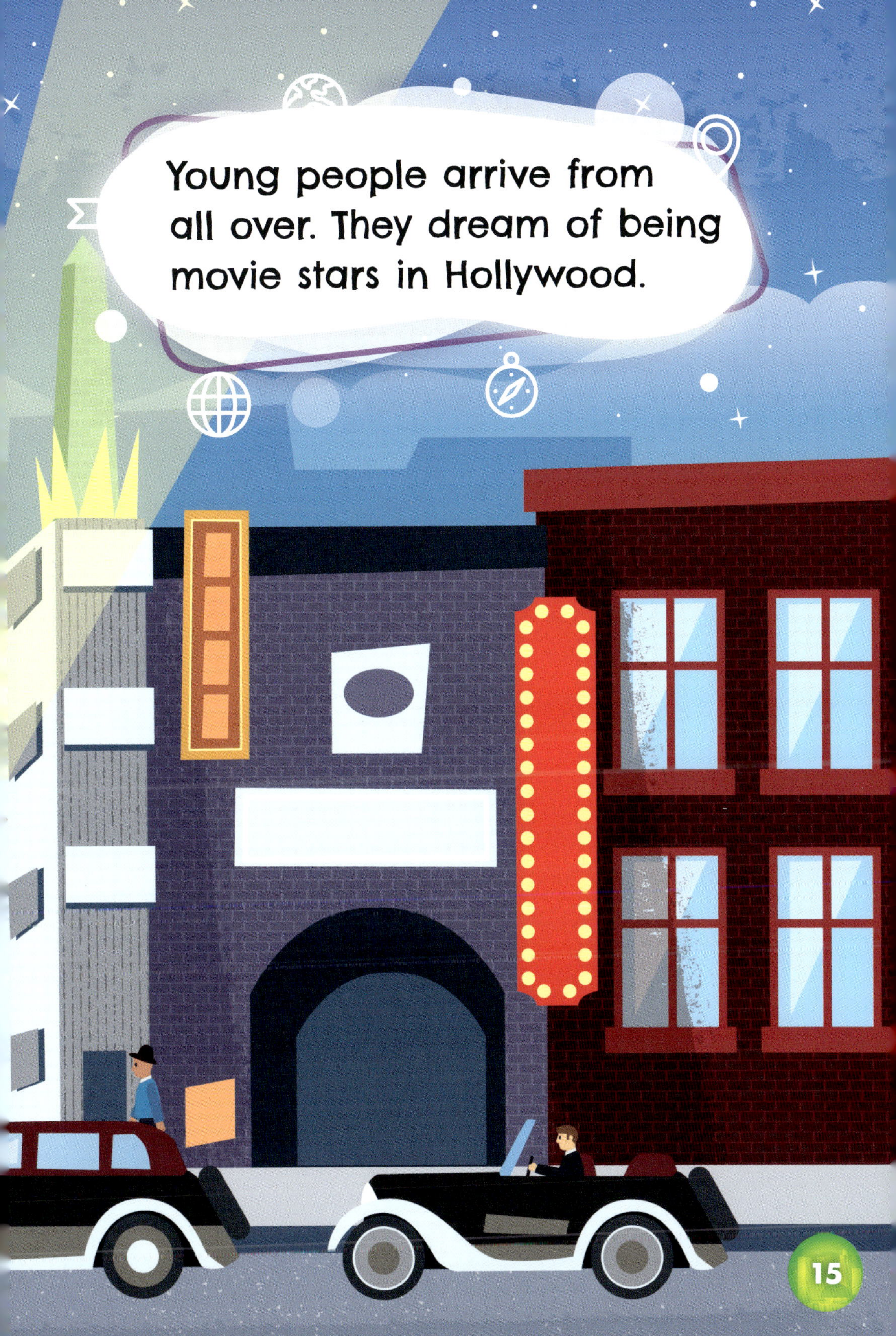

Young people arrive from all over. They dream of being movie stars in Hollywood.

1940s

World War II has begun. Los Angeles is growing fast.

Hundreds of thousands of people move here. They build aircraft and ships for the war.

1992

People are angry about a court **ruling**. They want **justice** for Black people. They burn buildings. They break windows.

The **riots** last for five days. Rebuilding the city will take a long time.

The City Today

People from all backgrounds live in Los Angeles. They watch sports and visit Griffith Park. They enjoy the warm weather.

Los Angeles and its people are full of history!

Los Angeles Timeline

1500s: The Tongva people live along the Los Angeles River in Yaanga village

1781: The Spanish government starts the town of Los Angeles

1821: Mexico wins independence from Spain and takes control of California

1876: A railroad connects Los Angeles to the rest of the United States for the first time

1920s: The movie business grows in Hollywood

1940s: Many people move to Los Angeles to build aircraft and ships for World War II

1992: Riots across the city last for five days

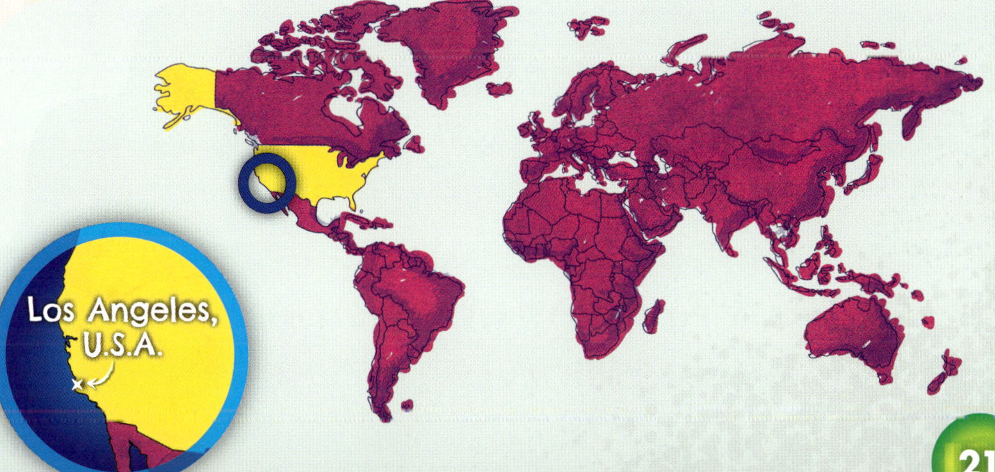

Glossary

governor–the leader of the government of a state

independence–freedom from being under the control of someone or something

justice–fair treatment

mission–a building where people do religious work; people in missions usually come from another country.

ranchers–people who work on large farms that raise horses, beef cattle, or sheep

riots–events in which large groups of people behave in an uncontrolled way

ruling–a decision made by a judge or jury in a court

World War II–the war from 1939 to 1945 that involved many countries

To Learn More

AT THE LIBRARY

Alexander, Heather. *Only in California.* Beverly, Mass.: Wide Eyed Editions, 2022.

Curlee, Lynn. *Trains.* New York, N.Y.: Atheneum Books for Young Readers, 2025.

Markovics, Joyce. *Los Angeles.* New York, N.Y.: Bearport Publishing, 2018.

ON THE WEB

FACTSURFER

Factsurfer.com gives you a safe, fun way to find more information.

1. Go to www.factsurfer.com.
2. Enter "Los Angeles" into the search box and click 🔍.
3. Select your book cover to see a list of related content.

BEYOND THE MISSION

> WHAT FACT FROM THE BOOK DID YOU THINK WAS THE MOST INTERESTING?

> WHICH PERIOD OF LOS ANGELES'S HISTORY WOULD YOU MOST LIKE TO VISIT? WHY?

> HOW DO YOU THINK THE DIFFERENT PEOPLE GROUPS THAT MOVED TO L.A. CHANGED THE CITY?

Index

aircraft, 17
beaches, 5
California, 5, 8, 12
Griffith Park, 20
Hollywood, 15
Los Angeles River, 6, 7, 8
Mexico, 10
mission, 8
movies, 14, 15
people, 5, 6, 9, 12, 13, 15, 17, 19, 20
railroad, 12
ranchers, 10, 11
riots, 19
ships, 17
Spain, 8, 10
timeline, 21
Tongva, 6
United States, 12
weather, 5, 13, 20
World War II, 16, 17
Yaanga, 6